SHIPWRECK REEFS

Aimée M. Bissonette

illustrated by
Adèle Leyris

Albert Whitman & Company
Chicago, Illinois

Splash! Kick!

Swim down into the deep.

Bubbles stream behind.

Sunlight filters through the warm, blue-green water, and a rippling curtain of butterfly fish skirts past.

Watch the fish move towards the ocean bottom—seventy feet, eighty—to a world of orange and pink, of colorful spikes and delicate loops, of darting fish and waving seagrasses…

...to a coral reef!

Coral reefs are formed by a simple relationship between two living things: algae and coral. Algae are tiny underwater plants that can float through the ocean. Coral are small animals that grow in large groups on hard surfaces. When algae and coral grow together, they form coral reefs. Reefs are safe, vibrant homes to thousands of sea creatures.

Reefs are underwater ecosystems. An ecosystem is a community of living things that interact with one another and all live in the same environment.

But somehow this reef is different from other reefs.

Look at its size and its shape—a long, bulky form resting in the sand, with railings, ladders, open doorways, and a broad, flat deck. A single mast rises up. It is crusted with sea creatures.

It's a sunken ship. One of many that litter the ocean floor all over the world.

This is a modern ship. The body of the ship, called a hull, is more than 300 feet long. It rests about 100 feet below the ocean surface in a part of the Atlantic where waters are warm. On a clear day, the ship can be seen easily from above.

COAST GUARD

This ship once sailed across the top of the sea. Now the ocean has claimed it as its own. Its size, its weight, and its steel body make it a perfect new home for marine life.

The ship is layered with algae, oysters, and barnacles—little crustaceans that fix themselves permanently to the ship's surface. Shy octopuses peek out from its nooks and crannies. This seagoing vessel is now an artificial reef.

An artificial reef is a coral reef formed from a man-made structure.

The ocean waters here reach average summer temperatures of 80°F. Reef-building corals grow best in water temperatures of 73–84°F.

It is hard to tell how this ship ended up here and how long it has rested on the ocean floor. There are many possibilities.

It may have sailed into a storm, been swamped by waves, or crashed on the rocks. Water would have rushed in and filled its hold, breaking it into pieces and slowly pulling it below the surface.

Many ships also go down in wartime. Warships from World War I and II are some of the best-known examples of shipwrecked reefs.

A German submarine from World War I houses a reef just off the coast of Yorkshire, England. It sunk more than 100 years ago.

The waters around Saipan, an island that was a Japanese stronghold during World War II, contain the remains of both US and Japanese warships, tanks, and aircraft.

Saipan's collection of sunken relics is now a maritime heritage trail, a protected area that includes nine dive sites.

People have also been making artificial reefs for centuries.

In the 1830s, ocean fishermen in South Carolina constructed artificial reefs out of logs. The logs attracted fish that were seeking shelter. When the fish grouped together around the logs, they were easier for the fisherman to catch.

Now, scientists can purposely sink ships in order to create new homes for marine life. The ship would have been stripped clean, had its doors removed, and then been towed out to sea, where explosive charges would have been set to blow holes in the hull and flood the ship.

Sinking a ship on purpose is called scuttling.

Holes are often cut in the ships before sinking so sea life can swim and crawl inside them more easily.

Sunken ships are newcomers to the deep sea. When a ship comes to rest on the ocean floor, it blocks the ocean's free-flowing water currents. The currents swirl around the ship as they flow past, carrying new life to it. This is how the ocean starts to build a reef.

Microscopic plankton get caught in the currents, spinning and rising around the ship's form. Sardines and minnows move in to feed on the plankton. Bluefin tuna arrive to feast upon the smaller fish. This is the start of a reef community and a new food chain. Sea animals live where they can find food. As smaller fish move into the sunken ship, bigger fish follow in search of a meal.

Plankton are small organisms that include crustaceans, like crabs or shrimp, and the eggs and babies of larger sea animals. Many animals rely on plankton for food, including sardines, minnows, shrimp, jellyfish—even whales.

Algae like living on hard surfaces, so they attach themselves to the ship's hull. Floating baby corals attach to the ship too. The algae and corals start their work as partners. Tiny algae live inside the corals, where they are safe from predators. The algae turn the sun's light into food for the corals.

At night, coral polyps extend their tentacles out to catch passing food.

The shipwreck reef becomes a feeding ground for sea creatures up and down the food chain. Tiny orange claw hermit crabs crawl among the reef's nooks and crannies in search of food. Loggerhead sea turtles dive down hunting for shrimp, crabs, and snails to eat. Rainbow parrot fish swim along dining on algae then tuck in for the night, wrapped in cocoons for protection from predators.

Loggerhead sea turtles are the world's largest hard-shelled turtles. They can stay underwater for up to four hours without air, searching for food in a reef.

Other creatures arrive seeking small, secret spaces—underwater cavities where they can hide. Longspine squirrelfish, red snapper, and snake-like moray eels shelter in the sunken ship. They snatch food swimming by and then dart back to the ship's dark insides.

Longspine squirrelfish are nocturnal and very territorial. They defend their underwater shelters by grunting and making staccato-like sounds.

Moray eels have very small eyes and don't see well, so they rely on their senses of smell to locate and ambush prey. They nestle into the dark cracks and crevices of sunken ships.

Silver-bellied yellow jack and sleek barracuda patrol the waters above the ship's deck, waiting for prey. Sharks circle the cracked hull, using their sharp senses of smell. They join the other apex predators searching for dinner. The ship supports a giant food web, feeding them all, big and small.

Apex predators are the top consumers in a food chain. They can prey on, or eat, nearly any other creature, and are not in danger of being eaten themselves. Sharks are the top predators in most marine ecosystems.

There are many kinds of artificial reefs. Objects that are made of steel, concrete, and other construction materials work well because they have surfaces corals can attach to easily.

The legs of retired oil and gas rigs in the Gulf of Mexico are blanketed in barnacles, corals, and underwater plants. Natural reefs do not form easily here. Natural reefs grow best in water that is shallow and warm. Here the water is cool and full of sediment, yet the artificial reefs thrive because they provide the missing hard surfaces for marine life in search of a sturdy place to call home.

Oil and gas rigs are platforms loaded with machinery that is used to drill into the ocean floor. When the supply of oil and gas below the ocean floor runs out, the rigs are retired and can be used as artificial reefs.

Thousands of subway cars have been used as artificial reefs too. Resting on the ocean bottom, these cars that once carried people are home to corals, mussels, and sea sponges, colorful sea animals covered in tiny pores. Sea bass and tuna swim through the subway cars' open doors.

From 2001 to 2010, more than 2,500 subway cars from the Metropolitan Transportation Authority (MTA) of New York City were stripped, cleaned, and sunk off the coasts of New Jersey, Delaware, Maryland, and South Carolina to create artificial reefs.

In the coastal waters of New Jersey, South Carolina, and Florida, divers explore artificial reefs made from sunken army tanks. The tanks, covered in puffs of soft corals, once rumbled through jungles and across deserts. Now they sit silently underwater, triggerfish and herring swimming around their turrets.

In the early 2000s, three different models of US Army armored vehicles were sunk as part of the New Jersey Artificial Reef Program. Some armored cranes were also sunk.

Whether a subway car or oil rig, army tank or shipwreck, artificial reefs do many jobs. Sunken ships are popular scuba diving destinations and lobster-fishing spots. As artificial reefs grow, they attract more fish, which means more tourists and fishermen come. That helps local restaurants, dive shops, hotels, and stores. A well-placed artificial reef also helps when severe weather strikes, by shielding the coastline from powerful wind and waves.

Artificial reefs are also important because natural coral reefs are fragile and are disappearing from our oceans. There are many threats to reefs, and most are caused by humans.

Careless scuba divers sometimes break coral when exploring. Overfishing, which is caused by people taking too many fish from one area too quickly, upsets the natural balance of the reef by removing key food sources.

Pollution and global warming are also threats to reefs.
Humans pollute, or contaminate, the ocean when they dump
chemicals such as oil, detergents, and sewage into the water.
Mountains of plastics enter the ocean this way too.

Humans are also causing the oceans to warm to unnatural temperatures by burning oil, coal, natural gas, and other fuels that produce the gas carbon dioxide, or CO_2. Too much CO_2 in the air contributes to warming temperatures. Some reef fish have started migrating north as they try to escape the effects of global warming, finding artificial reefs in cooler waters where natural reefs don't form.

When coral is negatively affected by things like pollution and warming waters, it can become stressed. This stress leads to bleaching, a condition where algae flee the coral polyps, causing the coral to turn white, stop growing, and sometimes starve.

Artificial reefs help ease the human activity at natural reefs by offering other locations for research, fishing, and diving. Artificial reefs can give natural reefs time to heal, which helps our oceans stay healthy.

Because reefs provide food and shelter for thousands of species of fish, invertebrates, sea turtles, dolphins, and whales, places for healthy coral to live are vital to the survival of a rich variety of marine life.

So dive in. Swim deep. Let the bubbles stream behind.
Follow the fish to that world of oranges and pinks.

Of staghorn, boulder star, and grooved brain corals.
Of purple reef fish, scrawled cowfish, and yellowtail snapper.
Of blue crabs, spiny lobsters, and leopard flatworms.
A world of sunken ships and coral reefs, a world of wonder in the vast, blue depths.

Remarkable, Resourceful, Artificial Reefs

When it comes to making artificial reefs, not everything works. There have been many failed attempts at creating artificial reefs. For instance, piles of old tires were once used to try to build reefs, but they did not work well because the tires leaked harmful chemicals into the ocean water that harmed marine life. They were also too lightweight to stay where they were put, and currents moved them along the ocean floor.

Many organizations and government agencies all over the world have set up programs to research, create, and maintain artificial reefs. In the United States, the coastal states of California, Texas, Louisiana, Mississippi, Alabama, and Florida all have artificial reef programs. Artificial reefs can also be found all over the world.

Here are examples of some creative approaches to artificial reefs:

Reef balls: Reef balls are man-made, hollow globes often made from concrete. Concrete is an excellent material for artificial reefs because it can be formed into nearly any shape, it's hard, and it's relatively inexpensive.

Underwater art exhibits: Artists around the world have made sculptures out of concrete that, once sunk, are both artificial reefs and underwater art exhibits. In the waters off Cancun, Mexico, there is an underwater art museum that hosts more than five hundred permanent pieces of sculptural art surrounded by swaying seagrass and covered in urchins.

The Museum of Underwater Art located near Australia's Great Barrier Reef opened in 2020 and includes an underwater coral greenhouse filled with twenty "reef guardian" sculptures.

Mineral Accretion Devices (MADs): Some artificial reefs called MADs are built with an added benefit to reef communities. They are made of metal and connected to a flow of low-voltage electricity powered by a windmill, solar panel, or generator. The electricity causes minerals to build up on the device when it is placed in seawater—the same minerals corals use to create their skeletons. The corals that attach to MADs grow three to four times faster than other corals, even in places where warming waters, bleaching, and pollution are a problem. Broken corals can also be transplanted from other reefs to recover on MAD reefs.

Additional Reading

Want to learn more about coral reefs? Here are some additional books you might enjoy:

Gibbons, Gail. *Coral Reefs*. Rev. ed. New York: Holiday House, 2019.

Hand, Carol. *Coral Reef Collapse*. Minneapolis, MN: Abdo, 2019.

Kopp, Megan. *What Do You Find in a Coral Reef?* New York: Crabtree, 2018.

Murphy, Julie. *Coral Reefs Matter*. Minneapolis, MN: Abdo, 2016.

For Maureen, whose love for snorkeling is unmatched in our family.
And, of course, with love to Bryan, Aliza, and Brian.—AMB

For my father, who gave me the travel bug
and taught me how to appreciate the wonders of the world,
whether they are above or underwater.—AL

Library of Congress Cataloging-in-Publication data is on file with the publisher.
Text copyright © 2021 by Aimée M. Bissonette
Illustrations copyright © 2021 by Albert Whitman & Company
Illustrations by Adèle Leyris
First published in the United States of America in 2021 by Albert Whitman & Company

ISBN 978-0-8075-1287-6 (hardcover)
ISBN 978-0-8075-1288-3 (ebook)

Printed in China

10 9 8 7 6 5 4 3 2 1 WKT 26 25 24 23 22 21

Design by Rick DeMonico

For more information about Albert Whitman & Company,
visit our website at www.albertwhitman.com.